THE ULTIMATE STARTUP GUIDE TO OUTBOUND SALES

How to Turn Cold Leads Into Hot Customers

By

Close.io Co-Founder & CEO, Steli Efti

THE ULTIMATE STARTUP GUIDE TO OUTBOUND SALES.

How to turn cold leads into hot customers.

Steli Efti

Copyright © 2014
Close.io, Elastic Inc.

Published by Close Publishing
501 Forest Ave
Palo Alto, CA 94301
www.close.io
Cover by Close.io
Printed in the United States of America

DEDICATION

To my mother Anthoula, my wife Diana and my little super hustlers Georgios and Leonidas.

Contents

Introduction

We launched our company because we saw too many startups with great products fail. Why did they fail? Lack of sales. We wanted to stop that. So we built an on demand sales team for technology companies that sell B2B. We helped more than 200 venture backed startups to close thousands of deals worth tens of millions of dollars.

We've helped startups at the discovery phase through the scaling phase. Consequently, we've helped them to figure out what works, build repeatable processes, and then amplify their results.

While we were doing all of this, we built a piece of software to help our sales reps called Close.io. We simply didn't like the sales software that was out there, so we built something that met our needs, something we truly wanted.

Our big advantage was that we worked with dozens of companies working in many different industries and verticals. Dealing with all these different scenarios helped us see the consistent and guiding principles of B2B sales for startups.

We know what makes outbound sales work. We

know it because we learned from the smartest sales experts in the Valley, took their advice and theories and tried them in the real world. Some of it survived the test, but a lot was simply good-sounding, but outdated advice. What you get in this book is real-world sales expertise.

Study it, use it and crush it.

Steli Efti, CEO of Close.io

STARTUP SALES BASICS

Inbound Or Outbound Sales – Which One Should You Focus On?

I share a lot of advice about outbound sales – thus many people naturally assume I'm an outbound advocate. I'm not. It's just one of the things I do, outbound is a part of the puzzle of success in business to me. But I don't think every startup should do outbound sales.

When it comes to inbound versus outbound, I'm not dogmatic – I'm pragmatic!

Fun fact: Close.io is doing zero outbound sales. All our growth is 100% inbound generated! There will come a time when we get outbound sales going, but right now we're too focused optimizing and scaling the inbound part of the business.

Cons of Outbound Sales

Outbound sales has taken a lot of flak – for several reasons…

Public Enemy Number One

Nobody wants to be cold called, even sales reps who cold call don't want to be cold called. I'm more receptive than most to cold calls because I'm a sales aficionado, I appreciate good salesmanship – but even I don't look forward to being pitched.

Interruption

When you're doing outbound sales, you're interrupting people. Everybody is an expert nowadays on filtering out interruptions. The average US citizen is bombarded with more than 2000 marketing and sales messages every single day (number varies depending on methods used to measure, but 2000 is actually the low end). It's like our brains have a subconscious TiVo or adware program running in our brain that immediately blocks anything that triggers the sales pitch alarm. You basically have to buy, beg or bug your way in.

High-pressure Sales Tactics

These are still commonly used and encouraged in outbound sales organizations – but you can (and should) be a smooth operator rather than a sales bully.

Time Inefficiency

Outbound sales reps waste a lot of time on mind-numbing tasks. They spend only a small part of their workday practicing their core skill: closing deals. (Which is something we're mitigating with our outbound sales software, but it's still a major pain point).

Finity

Outbound sales stops working as soon as you stop working. One of the big advantages of inbound sales is that it keeps generating leads even if you stop doing it. But as soon as you stop doing outbound, it stops generating new business.

<u>Pros Of Outbound Sales</u>

Now let's look at the flipside of the coin.

It Works

Yes, it's 2014. Yes, 'the buying cycle has changed', we're living in unprecedented times with social networks having changed the game of sales. But the fundamentals of salesmanship that worked in 1914 are still working now, and will still work 2114. Outbound sales brings home the bacon.

Predictable & Scalable

Once you have developed a sales process, you have a predictable, scalable growth mechanism for your business. Hire a new sales rep? You know how the actions you take now will affect your revenues three, six, nine months from now. Ask any business owner – that kind of simple formulaic predictability is a beautiful thing.

Power To Choose Your Customers

Outbound empowers you to pick your customers. Outbound is hunting – you pick a target and go for it. Inbound is fishing – you hang a fishing rod in the water and hope that a fish will bite, but your control over what kind of fish will bite is miniscule.

You Determine the Timing & Medium

Outbound sales gives you control to determine when you want to interact with prospects. This is the flipside of the "interruption" coin – rather than having to wait prospects to reach you through inbound requests when they are ready, you reach out to them when you are ready.

You also determine the medium of your interaction – be it an email, a phone call, meeting them at industry events or even knocking on their doors.

Immediate Results

Outbound sales can generate new business quickly, whereas inbound takes a long time to build up. If you want fast growth now, outbound is your friend.

Targeted Reach

If you're selling to professionals, outbound allows for much more targeted lead generation. This kind of laser focus allows you to execute with a higher level of precision and accuracy, and thus be much more effective. Want to reach the VP of marketing Citigroup? Good luck trying to get his attention with inbound tactics.

Higher Level of Engagement

The most impactful and influential sales outreach possible is a human one-on-one interaction. It allows you to truly engage with the buyer. Everything else pales in comparison when it comes to the impact you can have on an individual buyer.

Is Outbound Right For You?

It really depends on what the focus of your business is now, how fast you want to grow and what kind of business you want to run.

Your Strengths

Whether or not you've got what I call the "hustle DNA" and are a natural born sales person – you should be doing some outbound sales, just for the lessons it'll teach you. But don't try to force yourself and break your back over making outbound successful if you have other means for growth.

Your Market

Are there other companies doing outbound successfully? If yes, how are they doing it? Study their outbound sales process and learn from the market.

Your Results

Ultimately base your decision on the results you get. Outbound is probably the least trendy, hip, cool, awesome, amazing thing a startup can do to grow the business. But you're not in business to get admiration from your peers and the press, it's not a popularity contest.

Business is about the bottom line. The only thing that matters is: **does outbound sales make your business more successful or not?**

Lean Sales

Do you know what the best piece of sales advice in the world is?

Sell a good product -- something people want.

Since you're reading this book, you probably already have a product. But is it a product with real market potential? Will people want to buy it? Is there a feature that you could add that might turn your product into a breakthrough success? To answer that question, you need to get to know your potential customers. How do you get to know your potential customers? You do things the old-school way. Yes, we're running technology companies, but there's merit to doing things that don't scale early on.

1. Meet potential customers

Go out and talk to people who could be potential customers. Spend a whole afternoon walking into 10 different businesses, and say: *"Hi, I'm ..., can I talk to the manager/owner."* When you meet the owner, say: *"Hi, I'm an entrepreneur about to start a new business to fix a problem that I think you have. Can I get three minutes of your time to see if this is something that you might want?"*

This is the best way to get started. The big advantage here is that you're going to be able to get very valuable feedback, you're going to be able to see people's responses, it's very visceral, and you will get a real sense for how they run their operations. Although you can't do this kind of market research on a big scale, the quality of the responses/insights you get is really powerful.

2. Call potential customers

The next thing to do is to call potential customers. Even though you're missing out on a lot of visual clues about them and their business, you still get to have one-on-one conversations that will help you understand their wants and needs really well. This obviously scales a bit better than in person interactions.

3. Email potential customers

The next higher tier is to email people. You can email a lot more people, but the quality of the insights you get will be a lot different. You'll be able to see open/response rates and read people's responses. Written feedback often times is a bit more "filtered" than what people would tell you over the phone or in person. The great thing is that you can aggregate and analyze results at scale.

4. Separating real buying intent vs. "lukewarm interest"

When you're an entrepreneur just starting out, lots of people will tell you that your idea is great, just because they like you or want to encourage you. But there's a big difference between saying they would buy your product and actually paying money for it. How do you find out if they would have real intent to buy? One way to test this is to try selling your product even before you have built it.

Here's a simple question you can ask people to find out if they have real buying intent:

"What are all the steps I have to make for you to become my customer?" I call this the "virtual close".

Listen carefully, watch out for red flags and make sure you get a very specific answer. Once you've reached a point where the "virtual close" has occurred, do a test closing.

There are different approaches to do a test close, find one that works best for you:

- We want to start in 4 weeks - does this work for you?

- The beta program is heavily discounted. If you sign up now, you'll get it for half the price for life.

- What is the decision making process in your company? How quickly can we make a decision on this?

And then ask them for money. Tell them: *"Can I take your credit card info to process the payment?"*

Make it risk-free. Tell them their payment is 100% refundable, if they're not happy with the product, they can get their money back at any point.

Not everyone will be willing to give you money. But you can get at least some of the people who say they want your product to actually pay you in advance in order to get a discount in return or move the timeline up.

Summarizing the 4 steps to validate your Startup idea with sales:

1. Get a deep understanding of the environment your potential customers are working in by talking to them face-to-face.

2. Talk to more potential customers by

phone to see if the early problems you've discovered are validated with a larger test group.

3. Email more potential customers to test your early findings at scale/gather more data and build up a list of prospects.

4. "Test-close" prospects to determine whether they are just "curious" or real prospects with real pain points and willingness to buy your product/solution.

Charge Money for Things That Don't Exist Yet

I was talking to a good friend of mine who founded a very successful startup a few years ago and is currently considering a major new direction in their product.

He was asking me about my opinion on this new direction and the sales implications of going after a particular market with a very particular approach. As I was asking more and more questions to dig deeper into the matter he said one thing that raised an immediate red flag for me.

"We're getting a lot of interest for this but many potential customers want a key feature that we don't have yet, so we can't sell to them today. I think we're going to build out the product over the next few months, since we know exactly what the market wants, and then start selling!"

Beeeeep! Wrong answer!

The best way to discover if your product has a real market is to **SELL FIRST** and **BUILD SECOND.**

I told him what I always tell founders: *"You need to charge for the product today."*

No matter if it's ready or not. See here is the thing: **getting interest from businesses and getting customers is not the same thing**. Not even close.

You want to test interested parties to discover if they are true buyers with real buying intent.

But how do you do that when you know they need these key features that are missing? How can you charge for something that doesn't exist yet?

It's simple.

Give Incentives

They might not be able to benefit from the product/features they need right away (since you haven't built it yet), but they can pay upfront in order to receive one of 2 key benefits:

1. A massive discount for pre-ordering your product &

2. A shortened timeline for the feature/product release if they commit today

The Minimum Viable Pitch

Here's what you say:

"Alright dear interested prospect. It's clear that once we have feature XYZ we're going to be the perfect solution for you. We're planning to get that feature done and released in six months. The pricing will be around $$$ which would deliver [insert massive value] to your business."

"We want to give you the chance to get on the early customer list for this and gain some massive benefits. If you commit to make a deposit today for purchasing this product with feature XYZ in the future, we will give you a lifetime discount of 50% and we will move the development in our roadmap to be finished in 3 months instead of 6."

"The deposit is fully refundable so in case something unexpected happens to your business in the future you have no risk. Sound fair enough?"

Most Prospects Won't Bite and That's OK

If they are not interested in this deal chances are they are not a real early customer anyway.

Their pain is not big enough and their intent to purchase not strong enough to get them excited about these benefits.

But if you can't close 1 out of 5 or 10 prospective customers on this type of early-bird deal you're in trouble and might not really be on to something in the first place. You might want to spend a bit more time validating that there is a real demand for this product/feature before spending months and millions in feature development.

This Is Exactly How We Got Started

Here's a little secret: ElasticSales & Close.io started out like this. We sold our service before we were even able to deliver it, before our company even existed. You can listen to the whole story in my pioneers talk (skip to 3:44 in the video, that's where I start to tell the story of how we charged money for our sales on demand service before it even existed).

http://youtu.be/IfKMsdI9wJM

Fast Track to Product/Market Fit

The hardest (and most important) thing in the early phase of every startup is getting to product/market fit. Don't build and then sell. Do the reverse. Once you have people that gave you real $$$ in order to get the chance to buy your product earlier and for a discount you know you're really on to something worth building.

It's a simple strategy that will help you to get to product/market faster and with a lot less pain.

Selling Vision vs. Reality

As a founder, you have a vision for the potential of your startup: a successful company, a team of amazing people. You're working on an awesome product that solves your customers' needs better than anything else in the marketplace, and your customers love you.

Then, you open your eyes and look at what's there, now, in reality: a struggling startup, a crude and buggy first version of a product. Many features are lacking. The UI is just functional enough to let people use it.

This is relevant to startups that are out of the early product/market exploration phase that are growing their business. If your startup already has a viable product, paying customers, you're dealing with churn, and still have major product improvements on your roadmap that are going to take a couple of months to manifest - you'll need to balance the vision and the reality.

Focusing your pitch on the reality of your situation will stifle sales. However, when you sell too much of the vision, you will over-promise and under-deliver. Both of these scenarios are a recipe for disaster: a lot of unhappy customers.

Resist the Urge to Oversell

In a sales situation, you have to resist the urge to oversell on the vision. You will feel that urge because it's a cognitive bias that all successful salespeople possess: unbridled optimism.

You will want the deal to happen, and you'll be tempted to say anything to push the sale forward. Thus, your thinking will be skewed by default toward being too optimistic when assessing the situation: the product will be amazing – soon. Your next update will include all the missing features, and these iterations take no time at all in your imagination. In reality, you may be many months or years from delivering on your vision. This disparity between your sales promises and delivery will upset your customers and drive your project into the ground.

Sell the Vision - Just Not Too Much

You need to address the difference between what you have to offer now and what the customer wants in an ideal solution.

Are the crucial features going to go live within the next two to four weeks? If so, you can start selling them to your prospects. Simply inform them about the timeline, and let them decide if they want to begin using your product now so they can be ready when the updates come online.

Additionally, it's very important to deliver on the promise of bringing those new features to market as scheduled.

When in doubt, it's always best to under-promise and over-deliver. Tell the client you will have the features online in four weeks when you know you can have it done in two.

This way, they will be pleasantly surprised if you get it done in two, and they won't be upset if you find that you need the extra time and don't deliver until week four.

Don't Let Them Buy…Yet

Clients will appreciate the fact that you put off accepting their money until your product is ready to deliver the results they need. If it will it be more than two to four weeks before the features they need will be implemented, add them to your contact list for that update.

This is particularly important when you aren't sure whether you'll be able to release the update on schedule. Tell them, "No, this is not the right time for you to buy," then ask if you can contact them when the product is ready for their use.

Put them in your sales pipeline CRM, and keep them in the loop. Regularly let them know that you're making progress and how each update to your product will help solve problems for their business.

When you've released the features they want and need, you can go back and close the deal with these clients. They will appreciate your effort to deliver the services they need before taking their money.

This Is How You Get Brand Advocates

Customers who know that you have their best interests in mind will love you and recommend your products to others. You put their interest over your own, and they appreciate the effort. You didn't try to close the sale with them when it wasn't right, and they respect that commitment to their success.

Even some of the people who didn't buy will become advocates for your company simply because you are honest and forthright in your business practices.

In startup sales, it's important that you truly care for your customers – it's what pays off big in the long-run, and it's a strategy that bigger companies have a difficult time implementing.

Three Steps to Selling Vision and Reality

As a review, here are the three things you must do to properly sell your vision while basing the pitch within the reality of what your company has to offer now.

1. Start with the reality of where you are today.

2. Promise where you're taking your product tomorrow.

3. Give them some vision about where the product is headed in the next year or two.

Keep in mind that you must be realistic with your product offerings. When a customer wants you to deliver a service you are not prepared to offer for some time, refuse the sale. Stay in contact with these customers, and come back for the sale when your product has matured and you are comfortable delivering the services they need.

Pitchology 101

Giving a convincing sales pitch can be intimidating and complicated. Here's how to keep it simple and effective:

Focus on How You Say What You Say

When crafting a pitch, most people spend a lot of time and energy on the content and the words they use, but not enough time on how they deliver the message. Your body language and your tone of voice need to communicate enthusiasm and confidence.

Imagine somebody who doesn't understand a single word of English is in the room with you, watching you speak. That person should get the impression you believe in what you are saying, know what you are talking about and are enjoying talking about it. Make sure your body language and tonality make people want to listen. Practice in front of a mirror, in front of friends, or in front of a camera.

Get in the Zone

Feel great when you deliver the pitch. Most people feel negative towards selling or pitching an idea because they're anxious about the outcome. Do whatever is necessary to put yourself in a great emotional state before you deliver your pitch. Some people visualize their goals to feel inspired and upbeat. Some people work out. Others eat healthy food or listen to music they love and dance. Do what works best for you.

Ask to Understand

Want to know the real secret to success in sales? Empathy. You need to understand your customers' wants and needs, their challenges and problems, so you can help them in the best possible way.

How to gain this kind of understanding? By asking questions. Ask them about their work. Ask them about their situation. Ask them about their frustrations. Ask them about their ambitions. Do this until you know what they care about and understand what they need. Only then should you sell them the right solution, and only if it truly is the best solution for them.

Many years ago I attended a sales training that taught me the power of asking questions. It was the most important lesson I ever learned in sales.[1] This is what sales is about: ask the right questions. Listen.

Present Solutions, not Features

As a founder, you probably love the details of your product or service. But your customers aren't interested in your product. They are only interested in what your product will do for them: How will it solve their problems? How will it help them to achieve their goals faster and with less effort? How will it save them time or money? How will it protect them from risks?

Always translate your product's features into your customers' benefits. Don't focus on the bells and whistles, but what they do for them.

Manage Objections

Most people fail to prepare for objections. You want to identify the 10 to 20 most common objections and prepare answers to them. Your answers should be clear and concise.

Rehearse your answers until they roll off your tongue. When you encounter an objection in a sales conversation, you won't need to think

---

[1] You can read the full story behind this here
http://goo.gl/BIJGRX

about which words to use. Instead, focus on answering their question in a comforting manner. Keep eye contact. Nonverbally communicate expertise to create trust.

If you prepare for objections, you will look forward to addressing them. Most salespeople fear and try to avoid objections. Great salespeople do the opposite.

Ask for the Close

This step is all about confidence. Rehearse your close so you can deliver it smoothly. It should be a natural progression from your conversation, so that asking for purchase is the next logical step. Make your prospects feel as confident about your solution as you are. It's your job to guide your prospect through every stage of the buying process.

Negotiate

Once a prospect has made a buying decision internally, they will want to make sure to get the best deal they can. It's negotiation time. There are two simple rules to negotiating:

1. **Know your price.** Sometimes if it's necessary, you can offer a client better

terms or lower your price. But know your numbers in advance and decide at what point you just walk away from the deal. If a prospect can't afford to pay what you are worth, he's not the right fit. Be willing to walk away from the deal.

2. **Be quiet.** Use the power of silence to your advantage. Let the other side do the talking. If you keep your mouth shut at the right times, the client will often start to negotiate on your behalf. It's absurd and illogical, but it works.

Follow Up

Everything we have covered before now is just 20 percent of the sales process. Eighty percent of all deals are made in the follow-up.

Be consistent and reliable. Follow through on your word. Your margin of negligence in the follow-up is between staying true to your word and over delivering. Keep following up until you either get a yes or a definite no. But never ever interpret a lack of response or any other kind of message as a no. Winning in sales happens in the follow-up. Be relentless.

Anticipate Rejection

In sales, you often need to brush yourself off and keep on going. Dealing with rejection is a core skill. You need the emotional stability to take a "no" and still go into the next meeting filled with positive energy and enthusiasm.

The number of people who won't buy will always be larger than the number of people who will. You will encounter more no's than yeses. That's the way this game works.

Ask for Referrals

This is one of the most important steps to creating a truly scalable sales process. So make it part of your pitch. When a prospect has already made a buying decision, say: "Great, but I can't let you buy just yet. Right now, we are a startup. This means we focus all our energy, time and resources on delivering as much value as we can to our customers. We don't have a big marketing budget. If you are happy with our product, please recommend us to others who you think might benefit from our solution as well."

Put these 10 steps into practice and you will be able to craft and deliver an amazing sales pitch for your product, service or idea.

B2B Lead Generation

How should you source your leads for your outbound sales campaign? A lot of startups get this wrong – they either take the most obvious, easiest and least intelligent way, and it hurts their business, or they get caught up in fancy and clever ideas that sound great in theory, but don't produce results in the real world.

There are several providers that will sell you lists of names, emails, titles and other contact information and business data:

- Hoovers.com
- Data.com (formerly Jigsaw)
- Avention.com (formerly OneSource)
- zoominfo.com
- netprospex.com
- infousa.com
- etc...

Highest quantity/lowest quality: Buying Lists

If you buy from these providers, you should expect that a certain percentage of that data will be outdated. (It's been a couple of years since I last use any of these companies, but back then about 30%-40% of the data I bought was outdated).

Consider this will cost you twice: once the money you spend acquiring the bad data, and then the money (time/resources) you invest in reaching out to those unqualified leads.

High quantity/low quality: Web Scraping

An alternative to buying lists is to make your own list by scraping websites, which means you extract contact data from a website with a little program/script.

It's a bit of a gray area, and you should check if the website you want to scrape allows that.

If you target a very specific niche and there are highly targeted websites, this can be a successful approach.

Low quantity/high quality: Outsourced Lead Gen Team

Hire a company that manually finds leads for you, based on the criteria you establish with them. A good company to work with in this area is LeadGenius.com - they are a YC company and I've heard a lot of good things about them from different founders[2].

Lowest quantity/highest quality: Create Customer Profiles

Look at your current 5 most successful customers. Successful in this context means: a) they get the most value out of using your product and b) you profit greatly from them being a customer. (Look for the strongest win-wins between you and your customers).

And then try to identify the core DNA of your most successful customers. Ask a lot of questions about these companies and look for common denominators:
Look at your current 5 most successful customers. Successful in this context means: a) they get the most value out of using your product and b) you profit greatly from them being a customer. (Look for the strongest win-wins between you and your customers).

---

[2] Check out the Q&A they did with me: blog.leadgenius.com/sales-qa-steli-efti/

And then try to identify the core DNA of your most successful customers. Ask a lot of questions about these companies and look for common denominators:

- How big is the company?
- How many employees do they have?
- What other software tools do they use?
- What are the titles of all the employees?
- What kind of social media platforms do they use?
- Where are they located?
- What's their average deal size?
- How long have they already been in business?
- How did they hear about us? How did we acquire them?
- Etc. etc.

You'll have to ask a ton of questions and then filter out those that they have in common and that are most relevant.

Based on that you'll then create a very specific customer profile.

And then you go and find another 5 to 20 businesses that have the same core DNA (sometimes you can start with their closest competitors).

You don't need thousands of shitty names. You just need a handful of really great ones.

Reach out to those and strive to create high-quality sales conversations. Try to maximize response and conversion rates. Gain deep market insights that you can then leverage to make more sales and close better deals.

Find out what works best for you

You can probably tell from my answer that I personally prefer the highest quality, lowest quantity approach. But I encourage you to experiment for yourself. In some industries, for some businesses, the "spammy" high quantity/low quality approach works best.

How to Qualify Prospects & Leads

Qualifying is all about gaining the insights necessary to judge whether you should sell to a given prospect, and what is the best course of action to accomplish that is. Is this prospect a good fit for what it is you're selling? Is this a viable sales opportunity? And if yes, what's the best way to close the deal? Only after you've qualified someone can you really know whether investing your time and efforts into trying to sell to this prospect is worth it.

Many inexperienced sales people jump to the pitch too quickly, without having first gained a proper understanding of their prospect.

What Happens When You Don't Qualify Leads?

You're essentially throwing darts in the dark, operating like a mindless sales monkey. This will hurt your performance on several levels. You'll waste your time and energy chasing the wrong leads. You become a crocodile salesman - big mouth and no ears.

"Crocodile Salesmen are people who are always talking. They're pitching to you. They don't take the time to realize what your true motivations are because they're too busy telling you what they THINK you want to hear. Trust me – your chances of selling are much lower if you're talking rather than actively listening."

- Mark Suster[3]

Wasting Time

If you're not qualifying your leads properly, you'll waste a lot of time following up, and attempting to sell to prospects that aren't a good fit for your company. Spend this time on qualified prospects, and you'll close substantially more valuable deals.

Missed Opportunities

Sometimes the most difficult prospects can turn into the best customers. But how can you know whether this particular difficult prospect you're dealing with right now is one of those golden opportunities worth investing extra-effort into... or just wasting time?

[3] http://www.bothsidesofthetable.com/2010/02/03/the-danger-of-crocodile-sales/

You do it by asking the right questions that help you to gauge how much this opportunity could be worth, and how probable it is that they'll actually buy your solution.

Come up with questions that help you identify difficult, but valuable prospects.

Closing Bad Deals

Sometimes you might successfully sell to people who shouldn't buy your product. This isn't just bad for the customer who you persuaded into a bad buying decision - selling to the wrong customers is also bad for you and your company.

Not Knowing How to Sell to Them

What are their pain points? What's the context in which they evaluate your solution? What kind of person are you dealing with? What type of organization? If you don't know the answers to these questions, then you can't customize your pitch for them.

How to Close the Deal

What's their buying process? How long does it take this company to buy a product? What's the deal value? Not knowing these things can lead to bad "surprises". Most surprises you'll encounter in sales aren't actually surprises, they're just a result of a sales rep not properly qualifying a prospect.

How to Qualify

It's all about asking questions and eliciting the right information from the prospect.

There are four areas you want to focus on with your questions.

1. **Customer profile**
   How well do they match your ideal customer profile? How big is the company? What industry are they in? Where are your ideal customers located? What's the ideal use case? Which tools have they used in the past? What kind of ecosystem are they playing in? When qualifying prospects for our sales pipeline management software we ask people how many leads they usually have in their pipeline - if it's less than 100 a year, we recommend them to *not* buy our solution and instead just use a whiteboard or a spreadsheet.
2. **Needs**
   What are this customers' needs? Is it about reaching certain goals in

revenue? What are the needs of the individual, the team, and the company? When I interviewed Gary Vaynerchuk on how he is selling to Fortune 500 companies, he dropped some interesting insights on how B2B sales is fundamentally no different to B2C - you're selling to people, not companies. You have to know how to fulfill their wants and needs. What are the results they want to get? And how will those results affect them, their team and their company?

3. **Decision making process**
How do they make decisions? How many people are involved? Which departments are involved? What's their typical buying process like? How much time does it take them to buy a product? (Some organizations have 12 month purchasing processes - if you need to close deals in 3 months, that's no good for you.) When do they plan to buy? Maybe they're not ready to buy now, but will be in the future.

4. **Competition**
Who are you competing against? Which other vendors have they worked with? Are they evaluating your solution vs. building

their own solution? What are the criteria they base their decision on?

If you know all these things you'll have a really great idea if someone is a qualified prospect or not. Create a simple, one-page document that lists all the crucial questions you want to ask or the information you want to elicit.

How NOT to Qualify

While the most common problem is without a doubt that sales reps don't qualify their prospect well enough, there are also some people who take qualifying too far, and/or do it badly.

You can't just rapid-fire questions at your prospects. Qualifying is not interrogating, you need to be smooth about it. Weave the qualifying into the natural fabric of an engaging conversation, and approach the prospects with a sense of curiosity.

Identify Red Flags during Qualifying

During the qualifying stage there are several red flags you want to watch out for.

Spot Incongruences

Sometimes the answers you get from prospects don't paint a coherent picture. Some of the things they say don't fit together with other things they say, and you can't make sense of it all. Oftentimes they're giving you BS answers. Sometimes a prospect won't be completely forthright with you, and you want to recognize if they're giving you dishonest answers

Here's a common example:

A prospect will tell you that it's really important that your solution is scalable to many millions of customers. Later on you find out that their "team" is only two people (nothing wrong with that, been there, done that), they don't have venture funding, they don't have growth and they don't have customers. There's a bit of a disconnect when putting so much emphasis on scaling to millions of customers, and not having any at the moment. Maybe they are clueless and inexperienced, maybe there's something they are trying to hide.

Whatever it is - watch out for conflicting responses. Ask yourself if the story they tell you makes sense.

If it doesn't, then bring it up in a polite and honest way:

"I struggle with this little point, why is scaling so important if you are still small?"

Or: *"I'm struggling with this one piece of information, most of our customers who say XYZ don't have this constraint, why is this something that's important to you?"*

Just asking them to clarify will often be enough to bring up the real information.

Pay Attention to Context, Not Just Content

Don't just listen to *what* prospects say, but also to *how* they say it. If they tell you they're super excited about implementing your solution, but their voice is flat and muted... maybe they are not *really* that super excited.

When you notice this, give them opportunities to clarify things. Don't become inquisitive with them: *"Oh, you say you are super excited, but you sound totally bored, obviously you're not being honest here!"*

Simply say something like: *"Hey, a lot of times implementing a new solution is really hard. What are some possible issues you might encounter?"*

The point is to stimulate a real conversation, to get real information, and not just to comfortably cruise along the surface level.

The Reluctant Prospect

Sometimes prospects will exhibit an unwillingness to provide you substantial information. They'll repeatedly respond to your questions with "I don't know". Their answers will be so general and unspecific that they contain no valuable information.

If you're encountering a prospect like this, you're either

   a) talking to the wrong person and they're clueless, or
   b) they don't trust you.

Call them out on it. Tell them: *"We only deal with customers who become real long-term partners. To do that successfully we both need to be open. I really need to understand what you need in order to even judge if our solution is a good fit for you, or if I should point you into a different direction to make you successful."*

4 Signs of a Good Qualifying Process

There are certain things you can look at in your business that will be an indicator of how well you're qualifying prospects:

- Productive sales reps
- Successful customers
- A short time to close
- Good forecasting (knowing what kind of deals are going to close and what they are going to be worth).

What If Many Of Your Prospects Don't Qualify?

Sometimes you'll find that the vast majority of people you talk to simply aren't a good match for your product/service. If that's the case, you're probably casting your net too wide, and should consider a more focused and targeted approach to lead generation. There's no point in spending most of your time with prospects who will never buy.

COLD EMAIL

Get Started With Cold Sales Emails

One of the biggest challenges in B2B sales is reaching the right person - the person who can:

a) understand the value your software can provide for their company and

b) make a buying decision.

Salespeople and lead generation teams generally waste too much time on this task. Your company can create a lot more high-quality leads in less time by using cold emails based on Aaron Ross' predictable revenue model.

(If you haven't read his book Predictable Revenue, you should do this now. It's the one book

When we talk to many B2B startup founders, they get it. They recognize that cold emailing could make their outbound prospecting more effective. But they don't know how to get started implementing it into their sales process.

Let's look at these six simple steps to getting started with cold emails:

1) Write your subject line.

It's just one line, but it's the line that matters most. If people don't open the email, nothing else matters. There are many things you can do to increase open rates, but one easy best practice is using their name in the subject line.

2) Write your email copy.

Be brief. Give context. End with a clear and specific call to action. Every sentence is sealing the value proposition of giving you a bit more of their time and reading the next sentence you wrote. (Remember: most email clients display not just the subject line in the inbox, but also the beginning of the email copy).

3) Get feedback.

Show your outbound cold emails to different people, especially current clients of yours with whom you have a good relationship. Ask them: "Would you reply to this? What's unclear? What would you change?" If you have investors, ask them the same questions. Get feedback. Edit/Iterate/Test.

4) Send 25-50 emails a day.

Don't blast out hundreds (or even thousands) of emails when you're just getting started. Your goal here is to find out what works, while at the same time having enough resources to follow up properly with those prospects who respond. You probably already know how to find almost anybody's email address.[4]

5) On the following day, look at these two metrics:

- a) Open rates (benchmark: 15-30%)
- b) Response rates (benchmark: 10-30%)

6) Iterate.

Try different subject lines and different email body. Experiment and measure results.

If your response rates are below 5% you're doing something really wrong. In the 10% range you're on the right track. Anywhere between 10%-30% you're doing really, really well.

---

[4] https://www.distilled.net/blog/miscellaneous/find-almost-anybodys-email-address/

Subject Lines That Get Emails Opened

The subject line is the most important part of any email, especially if it's a cold sales email. If your subject line fails to get the recipient to open the email, everything else you do doesn't matter. If an email isn't opened, it didn't exist.

Here some simple ways to craft subject lines that compel recipients to open the emails. Don't think of them as rules – think of them as useful data to base your own experiments on. Some of these work better than others in certain markets and for certain companies – the only way to find out which is right for you is to experiment.

Write like a human being

Make it read like it's written from one person to another. Not like it's written by a marketing department to a prospect. Just someone writing an email to someone else, in a conversational tone, not business jargon.

Don't write fancy formatted emails filled with marketing speak. It's not a newsletter. You know how many newsletters people get every day? It's adds up to about a bazillion. It's the first thing people delete or archive unread when skimming through their inbox. That's not what you want to happen to your email.

Avoid catchy slogans

I could send you an email with the subject line: "Close.io Best New Innovation In CRM In Ages". Many people think a "business email" is supposed to look like this. But if you want to get your emails actually read, avoid it.

Lower caps

Don't capitalize every word. Even though it might formally be the right thing to do, writing in lower caps increases email open rates. Probably because when people write an email to someone else, they often don't capitalize each word.

Subject line only emails

Send out emails with only a subject line, no email body text. Using EOM[5] at the end of your subject line also works well. I know a sales team that's killing it with this technique.

Use their name

A simple and widely used element of successful subject lines is including the recipient's first name.

You might even want to experiment with ONLY using the first name in the subject line. If I'd get an email in my inbox with the subject line "Steli", I'd probably open it. The same thing applies to using the company's name.

Misspellings

This is a subject line hack that few people use - but using a misspelling can actually increase

---

[5] http://lifehacker.com/5028808/how-eom-makes-your-email-more-efficient

open rates. Slapdash misspellings that indicate you were typing it hurriedly are a better choice than those that indicate you don't know how to spell.

Example:

- "Steli, cna we meet today?" (tells the recipient you hurriedly typed it in)
- "Steli your invited to join us" (tells the recipient you don't know the difference between you're and your)

Questions

Questions in subject lines increase open rates. Asking the right questions is an art, and the better you get at it, the more you sell. Use the power of questions in your subject lines as well.

Your first sentence

Most email inboxes nowadays actually display the first sentence or so of the email body in addition to the subject line. This is another opportunity for you to get your email opened, and you should craft it with your subject line in mind.

Keep your promises

Once you start getting creative with subject lines, it's easy to get tempted to go too far. Certain subject lines might get you amazing open rates - but you need to not just look at this one metric, but the overall funnel. A lot of cold emailing nowadays is done with the "Re: " subject line, implying that there's been a previous conversation.

But your email body should deliver on what your subject line promises. If you mislead people to get an email opened, they'll read your email and delete it. Nothing gained from that.

One of the most effective attention-getting emails I got was the subject line "Steli, I'm disappointed".

I immediately clicked on that email, and then it went on saying basically: "I'm disappointed that we weren't able to connect. What we're doing is... blablabla..." and the email went straight into the pitch.

That email was like a guy running a marathon, and sprinting the first three miles, being ahead of everyone else... and then collapsing and never making it to the finish line. It was the first email that I opened in my inbox, but once I saw that the subject line was just a clever trick, and the sender wasn't really disappointed, I didn't bother responding.

4 cold email subject lines that get open rates of +35%

1. "Introduction: {Name}" or "Introduction {your name/company} <> {their name/company}
2. "quick request"
3. "Trying to connect"

4. "{name of their company}"

2 Bonus Tips for Effective Cold Emails

Timing

If you're doing cold emailing professionally, you probably know about common best practices. Statistics show that the best time to send emails is around 8 or 9 am (local time of the recipient) on Tuesdays and Thursdays.

That's exactly why you should experiment with doing something else. Because so many people are following these best practices, and come Tuesday 9am prospect's inboxes are flooded with dozens of cold emails and newsletters.

Try the contrarian approach and send out emails at odd times. Weekends? Or 5:30 am? Or super-late. Experiment to see if odd timing can lift your response rates.

Sent from my iPhone

Just add this little line underneath your signature. We used this a lot when we were running Elastic Sales, and consistently saw a large increase in response rates. Even with autoresponder emails and drip campaigns. Consider if you want to use this - it feels a bit deceptive, but it's very effective for most audiences.

Cold Email Templates

Every company is different but these cold email templates and best practices should be a good starting point for most of you.

There are 2 approaches to cold emails used today:

1. You're emailing someone high up in the organization asking for a referral down to the right person (aka Cold Calling 2.0)[6]

2. You're emailing the decision maker directly pitching them to sign up/call/meeting/etc

Let's get started with cold email templates asking for referrals within the organization:

---

[6] http://www.forentrepreneurs.com/predictable-revenue/

Cold Email: Referral V1

Hi [first name],

My name is [My Name] and I head up business development efforts with [My Company]. We recently launched a new platform that [One Sentence Pitch]

I am taking an educated stab in the dark here, however based on your online profile, you appear to be an appropriate person to connect with... or might at least point me in the right direction.

I'd like to speak with someone from [Company] who is responsible for [handling something that's relevant to my product]

If that's you, are you open to a fifteen minute call on _____ [time and date] to discuss ways the [Company Name] platform can specifically help your business? If not you, can you please put me in touch with the right person?

I appreciate the help!

Best,

Sig

Cold Email: Referral V2

Hi [first name],

I hope I'm not bothering you. Could you please refer me to the person in charge of [Something that's relevant to my product]?

Thanks for your time,

Sig

Cold Email: Referral V3

Hey [first name]

My name is [My Name] and I'm with [My Company Name]. We work with organizations like [Company Name] to [insert one sentence pitch].

[One sentence unique benefit].

Could you direct me to the right person to talk to about this at [Company Name] so we can explore if this would be something valuable to incorporate into your events?

Cheers,

Sig

The next referral cold email is a template directly from the team at predictable revenue[7]:

Subject: Can you point me in the right direction?

Hey [first name],

I'm sorry to trouble you. Would you be so kind as to tell me who is responsible for [insert your biggest pain point here that resonates with your ideal customer; OR insert function like "sales" or "recruiting"] and how I might get in touch with them?

Thank you,

Sig

---

[7] http://predictablerevenue.com/

Let's check out 2 cold emails that are using approach #2 and pitching the decision maker directly on the value proposition and next action steps:

Cold Email: Selling V1

Hey [first name],

I hope this email finds you well! I wanted to reach out because [explain how we got their contact information and how we relate to them: talked to a colleague, saw your company online, etc...].

[Name of Company] has a new platform that will help: (your team at) [Organization Name]. [One sentence pitch of benefits]. We do this by:

• Benefit/Feature 1

• Benefit/Feature 2 [optional]

Let's explore how [name of your software] can specifically help your business. Are you available for a quick call [time and date]?

Cheers,

Sig

Cold Email: Selling V2

Hey [first name],

I hope this email finds you well! I wanted to reach out because [explain how we got their contact information and how we relate to them: talked to a colleague, saw your company online, etc...].

[Name of Company] has a new platform that will help: (your team at) [Organization Name]. [One sentence pitch of benefits].

I know that [our product] will be able to help [name of your company] [insert high level benefit here].

Are you available for a quick call [time and date]?

Cheers,

Sig

COLD CALLING

The Successful Sales Call Blueprint

When selling on the phone, often times the problem sales reps have (or non sales people trying to sell) is they don't understand how to structure a call. If you don't have the right plan going into a sales call, it's going to be much harder to close the deal.

Every sales call, from a cold call until a closing call, should follow a pre-planned structure that is meant to optimize the likelihood of a desired result. That doesn't mean there can't be detours along the way. It's analogous to driving somewhere new the first time – you will almost always use Google maps to give you a plan and direction. Then, each proceeding time you might use your directions a little less. A sales call, at any stage of the process should include these five steps:

Step #1: Introduction

The goal of the introduction is very simple – talk to the prospect and get them in the right frame of mind. Create context and build rapport. Make sure they are present and engaged in the conversation before attempting to pitch anything.

Examples:

- *Did I catch you at a bad time?*

- *Do you have 'x' in front of you?*

Step #2: Questions

If this is a first sales call, this is where you qualify the prospect. In later sales calls, this is when you ask deeper qualifying questions and do discovery in order to find out what has changed / happened since the last call and what the current status is.

Examples:

- *How are you currently doing 'x'?*

- *What did your team think of the proposal you and I talked about on our last call?*

Step #3: The Pitch

You've had a successful introduction and asked all the important questions to reach real understanding of your prospect. This is the part of the conversation where you offer your pitch. The pitch is not always going to be selling your entire product; rather it is going to be selling them on the objective of the call (i.e. a follow up

call, an in person meeting, or a demo or a close).
Your 'questions' should help prepare you for the
pitch.

Examples:

- *We are going to streamline your process
  by…*

- *We are going to save you 'x' dollars each
  month by…*

- *We can solve your security challenge by...*

Step #4: Managing Objections

A prospect almost never bites on the pitch with
no questions or concerns. So, during this part of
the call you anticipate objections and manage
and address them. Learn here how to manage
any objection successfully!

Examples:

- This is something I hear pretty frequently,
  but here's the thing…

- I hear you. Most of our customers had
  the same concern. Let me tell you how
  we're addressing this today...

Step #5: Next Steps

Finally, all sales calls should end with next steps and action items. If you don't have action items (i.e. another call or a check in after the client is using the product), then you will be facing an uphill battle next time you talk with the prospect.

Examples:

- *When are you going to be able to bring this back to your team?*

- *When is a good time for us to connect again?*

The above five steps provide a great starting point for a sales rep of any experience. Now, try making it your own and see how things improve.

Create a Sales Phone Script

A phone call can be an incredibly effective tool to reach out to potential customers and close deals. How do you know that you have a sales pitch that is effective on the phone?

Prepare and write a structured phone script.

Let's look at a simple cold call script structure you can use:

#1 Raise curiosity (who is this? why should I care?)

#2 Give context (elevator pitch)

#3 Ask for permission to continue

#4 Ask questions. Learn about their needs. Define if they are a fit

#5 Test close: Price sensitivity, Timeline, etc

#6 Schedule next steps

Opening:

#1

Hi, my name is_____. I'm calling some startups in the area to find out if they are a good fit for our product/service/beta program.

#2

What we do in a sentence is we provide companies with xyz.

#3

Does this in general sound interesting to you?

#4

Qualifying:

What is your current xyz process?

Who are your customers? How do you currently solve xyz?

Etc.

#5

Test Closing:

We would want to start in X weeks - does this work for you?

The beta program is heavily discounted. It's going to be $X/day per.

What is the decision making process in your company?

Etc.

#6

Next Steps

Great. Sounds like this could be a good fit. Let me send you our brochure and schedule a time next week to discuss all your questions etc.

What's the best email to send you information and the cal invite?

What's a good time to chat next week?

Cold Calling Conversion Funnel Metrics and Benchmarks

If you are a startup that's doing cold calling, you're always trying to get better results.

At least twice a week I'm talking to founders who want to know how to improve their outbound phone sales approach by describing to me their basic input/output metrics.

They'll say *"We're closing an average of 1 out of 100 leads we call. How can we improve this?"*

That's an impossible question to answer. You can't just look at input/output and know how to optimize or were the issues are. You need to understand the entire cold calling conversion funnel.

Look at your entire cold calling conversion funnel:

1. How many leads do you have?

2. How many calls do you make?

3. How many decision makers do you

actually reach? (reach rate)

4. How many of the people you reach are actually qualified to buy your product?

5. How many of these qualified opportunities do you close?

Once you have these numbers, you're much better equipped to **decide which part of your funnel needs improvement**. You want to fix the part of the funnel first that will make the biggest difference to your bottom line. Usually you want to start at the top of the funnel and look at the quality of your leads and the average reach rates you're getting.

Improve your reach rate:

One of the main inefficiencies of cold calling that people don't take into account is **reach rates**. (That's why we encourage you to call every signup within 5 minutes for inbound leads).

In cold calling there often is no quick fix to improve this number. If you talk with people who do cold calling, you'll find that about 90% of their efforts are wasted on just trying to reach decision makers. Even slight improvements in your reach rate will yield significantly better results for your overall cold calling conversions.

Reach Rate Benchmarks: 15% or higher

These numbers refer to how many decision makers you reach (not gate keepers):

- 10% or less = you're toast

- 15% = you're doing ok, this is pretty much standard

- 30% = you're doing great!

Qualify more leads:

The next common problem in your cold calling funnel might happen at the qualifying stage. If you qualify only a low percentage of people you reach, that means you're calling bad leads (or less likely you don't know how to qualify people in the first place).

You probably need to have more narrow definitions of your target market and hence setting more criteria on what constitutes for a good cold calling lead.

Qualifying Benchmarks: 50%.

This might seem high, but if you have good

leads, then you should qualify around half the people that you reach. If you qualify less than 50%, you need better quality leads.

To clarify, a qualified lead is a decision maker that you had the chance to talk to and ask the basic questions that would lead you to confirm that they actually should buy your product because they are a good fit. If you reach a decision maker but they hang up immediately that doesn't make them unqualified but rather decreases your reach rate.

Close more deals:

If your Reach-To-Qualify ratio is good, but you don't close enough deals, you have a few basic options:

1. You don't have product/market fit yet

2. Cold calling is not a viable way to sell your product/service

3. Your pitch sucks

Look at the way you're selling and evaluate if the pitch is sound. Have outside experts (other founders/sales executives or investors) come in and evaluate your sales approach. If your pitch is good, you're likely having problem number 1 or 2 (no product/market fit or cold calling isn't viable for you).

Closing Rate Benchmarks: 25% - 30% = you're good.

If you close less than 25% of the people who qualify, you're probably in trouble.

Discover how to fix your funnel:

In general it's best to start at the top of the funnel because these numbers will affect everything else that happens later on. Look at the benchmarks simply as a way to identify when to move down to the next step in the funnel, and keep in mind that the percentages might differ depending upon the specifics of your business.

Simply saying *"How can we improve sales?"* is not enough. You need to know your cold calling funnel to understand what's going on and spot real opportunities for improvements.

Afraid Of Cold Calling? Turn Your Fear of Failure into Fearlessness

Entrepreneurs often struggle when they start doing cold-calls. They hate calling others to drum up business and they're not good at it either. Their approach is too timid and they give up too soon when they encounter resistance. They don't manage objections well. And they don't bring home the bacon at the end.

Fear of Failure

One of the guys on our team had this problem which was strange, because he was an audacious, bold and outgoing person. But tell him to sell on the phone, and he turned into a frightened little chicken.

The cause was obvious: *fear of failure*. He was scared of rejection. We both knew it. He also rationally understood that this fear did not serve a positive purpose, yet, he was stuck in it.

Turning Fears into Reality

How could we get him unstuck? How could we shake him up and change his state?

I decided to challenge him with a new task.

"Fail with every call!" For the rest of the day, he should call people and make them hang up on him. His mission was to fail miserably.

To make it more fun, I told him fail in a different way with each call. "Start with speaking painfully slow and unenthusiastic", I told him.

Our little coaching conversation had turned into the center of attention in the office. Everyone on our team was looking at him when he made the first call. His discomfort was obvious. But he played along. Each... word... spoken... sloooowwwwlyyy... with... excruciatingly... looong... silent... pauses... in between. *Painful.*

Everyone in the office had to tap into the core of our brains self-control center not to burst out laughing. But there was no holding back once the other person hung up on him. The whole office was going crazy, including him.

The team came up with a new challenge for the second call: stuttering. "Hell hell hell hello, thi thi this is is is..."

After ten of these calls the atmosphere in the whole room had totally changed.

Changing Your State

I looked him in the eyes and said: *"Now go and fucking get'em. Close deals. Take everything you got and make it happen! And have fun!!!"*

Suddenly he was a different person. Total transformation of energy: fearless and unstoppable. A relentless machine.

What caused this transformation?

Not a new insight. He already knew that it was just fear holding him back. But he had now transferred that insight from a logical, rational level into an instinctive insight. He had emotionally internalized what he knew mentally by making failure real. And that led to the breakthrough in his behavior.

Use this technique if you ever feel anxious about cold calling (or use it to help a colleague).

1. Address the issue and verbalize it.

2. Instead of trying to avoid failure, aim for failure.

3. Be creative about different ways to successfully achieve failure.

4. Have fun and be silly. It will unlock the secret vault of sales power deep inside of you.

5. Now that you have experienced what failure feels like, realize there is nothing to be afraid of

6. Now crush it and see how you can perform once you aim for success.

IN THE MIDST OF SELLING

Manage any sales objection successfully!

Most sales reps are coming up with answers to objections on the fly. **That's a huge mistake.**

What you need is to develop an **objection management document.** I'll share with you how to do that in a few simple steps.

But first let's look at all the reasons why "computing" an answer to an objection in real time is a bad idea:

1. It's going to take focus/attention away from the customer while you're trying to formulate your response

2. It's going to probably be a much longer answer than you want to because you're just communicating in a stream of consciousness

3. You're not going to seem very confident

4. The quality of your answer will heavily depend on your state at the present moment

So how do you create a great objection

management doc?

Here are the 5 simple steps:

1. Write down the top 25 objections you're facing in your market

2. Write down the best answers to each objection

3. Limit the answers to a max. of 3 sentences

4. Have at least 10 people review the answers with you and give feedback

5. Train your team/ yourself to know these answer by heart

What are the benefits of doing this?

There are many benefits in doing this exercise and creating an objection management doc but by far the biggest one is the **boost in confidence** it will give you & your team when delivering the answers.

Here are a few common objections to get you going:

- I don't have time

- I don't have money

- Your product/service is too expensive

- Please just send me more information

- We don't need this

- {add more industry/market/product specific objections}

The Virtual Close

Lots of founders come to me for advice on big deals that they're trying to close.

A lot of times they describe how they met with a buyer from a huge corporation,demoed their products, answered all initial questions, and seem to be getting some good buying signals.

They just finished their first really good initial meetings and then send follow-up emails to schedule the next face-to-face—and now they enter uncharted territory.

They worry:

- Is this deal really realistic?
- What do I need to do next to make this happen?
- Are they really interested or just being nice to us?
- How long will this take?
- When and how should I follow up? Should I wait until they get back to me or be proactive? If so how much?

At that point, I ask them if they took the chance to actually have the potential customer describe to them in detail what it will take for them to become a customer. Most of them say no. And that's the problem.

The solution to this is something I call the "virtual close."

This sales tactic will help you accomplish these objectives:

- Figure out the roadmap of all the steps its going to take to close the deal
- Discover major red flags and issues that will slow the deal down or prevent it from happening
- Guide your prospects or their internal champion—someone within a prospect's company that's on board but needs to convince others—through all the steps he or she will have to take to make the deal happen
- Make your prospect imagine and visualize a future where he or she has become a customer of your product or service
- Uncover whether there is no real buying intent

How? Simply ask this question:

"Dear potential customer. Now that you know what we do and we answered all your questions, it seems to me that we are a perfect fit. What are all the steps we have to take to help make this happen?

Then shut up and listen.

If the prospect says something to the effect of:

"Well, not sure..." or "Well, we wouldn't buy before 2023 since we are locked in the current contract…"

You're in trouble. This means there is no real buying intent. Move on with life.

In all other cases, you have to put on your investigative hat and actually keep following up with questions until you both reach a point where a deal can happen.

Here's what a typical conversation should look like:

You: "Dear customer. What will it take for you to buy our product?"

Customer: "Well, I would have to show it to my boss and some colleagues and see what they think."

You: "Great. How do you typically get feedback?

Scheduling a meeting? This week? Next week? Do you make a presentation or how does this typically work?"

Customer: "Well, we have a weekly standup meeting and that's when I will present this."

You: "Awesome. What happens when your boss and teammates really like the idea and want to move forward?"

Customer: "Then we would schedule a follow up call with you and all stakeholders to answer all questions."

You: "Makes sense. Let's assume we have a great call and I can answer all questions to the teams satisfaction and we're all happy to move forward. What happens next?"

Customer: "Well, then it would have to go through legal."

This is the point where most people would stop asking questions and feel happy about what they have learned. That's a mistake. Keep asking questions until you've arrived at the virtual close. Like this:

You: "Of course. How does this process typically work for you? Have you purchased something similar to our product in the past six months and can you describe to me what we'll have to do to make the process as smooth as possible?"

Customer: "Yes, we'd have to run through a few higher-ups, then the purchasing department and ethics committee."

You: "Oh interesting. Could you describe this process a little more?"

Customer: "Well, purchasing usually takes a couple weeks to review, and if it looks good, then they move it on to ethics, who has the final sign off."

You: "Great. But THEN we're in business right?!?"

Customer: "YES!"

Now you know what it will take to make this happen. You have a roadmap to:

- Forecast accordingly
- Start preparing all steps and run some of them in parallel to save time
- Decide if you really want to pursue this deal

On top of that, you've made them create a world where they are customers and have already made a small mental commitment to it.

After this conversation, you'll have all the information you need, the customer has thought through the deal—and you have everything you need to make good decisions and make every deal happen.

Sell To "Non Believers" - Turn Doubt into Trust

"Our product works. It saves our customers a lot of money. We can prove it. Heck, we even do a pilot for them when they ask. Afterwards, they see the numbers, the data confirms our claims. ***But they still don't buy!*** *What are we doing wrong?* "

This is the main sales challenge of a startup I recently talked to in a sales office hour.

Their product is strong. They're serious players; big government agencies among their customers (and they showcase it on their website).

They think they've arrived at the promised land of product/market fit.

Their business is doing very well, through referrals. But now they want to grow faster, so they started a cold outreach campaign.

Generating qualified leads is easy for them. They reach decision makers and get them to listen. They even get them interested. Companies actually *want* what they offer.

The Sales Process Is Moving Along Nicely

They've got a qualified prospect. The decision maker wants a demo. So the do a demo for her. The product does everything they claimed it would. Everything the prospect wants.

But she still doesn't buy.

Why?

Let's summarize the situation:

- You have a great product.

- People want what your product does. And you can prove it.

- But they still don't buy. Even after you showed them that buying would be the logical thing to do. WTF?!

If you have dealt with objections on a logical level and they still don't buy... let's look at the emotional level.

What's the issue?

Doubt! *They're scared to make a mistake. They're afraid of being wrong.*

They *logically* know that it makes sense to buy

your product.

But what if they sign the deal and something goes wrong? It would fall back on them. It puts their career and reputation at risk. Why should they stick their neck out and take the risk?

It feels dangerous! Like skydiving. You *know* the equipment is working. You *know* the parachute will bring you down to earth safely. *But boy is it fucking scary when you're looking out of the plane…*

These fears are not purely rational. You cannot resolve irrational fears with rational arguments.

If a prospect has irrational fears related to your offer, and you try to address those with rational arguments, what will happen?

The prospect will make up bogus objections, because they don't want to be perceived as an irrational person. And then you have to deal with those bogus objections — and that's a fight you can't win.

So what do you do instead? If you can't use rational arguments, how do you overcome irrational objections?

There are three things you do:

1) Sell on 3 levels

I see this all the time in companies that have a strong product: they sell only the product.

But **the product** is just one level you need to sell.

What are the other two levels?

You need to **sell yourself** as someone who is trustworthy.

And you need to **sell the company** as a business that is stable, growing and winning in the market. You need to make them believe your company will still be around in two, three, five years.

Your prospect most likely isn't a product person. She often doesn't have the technical expertise. She hasn't spent years developing and building products. She doesn't even understand how your product works exactly. *How can she trust something she doesn't fully understand?* You need to make her trust in your sales rep (a human being) and your company (a group of human beings).

This is not necessary in *every* industry, but in *some* industries it is *essential.*

2) Address the Elephant in the Room

Do they have an objection they don't feel comfortable bringing up? Good! This is your opportunity to bring it up!

Most sales reps try to stay clear of latent objections if the prospect doesn't bring them up.

Instead, what you want to do is to pull this hidden objection out of the dark, put it in the middle of the room, shine a big bright light on it and kill it in front of your prospect.

How exactly do you do that?

Preparation. Identify what exactly scares them. Make a list of the three most common fears prospects have regarding your product.

Then you say:

"I know what you're thinking. You're thinking 'This thing really works. Now I actually have to consider purchasing it.' That can be a scary thought, right? You're skeptical about [fear 1], [fear 2] or [fear 3], right? That's completely normal. I encounter this every time. That's how

every single of my customers felt at first."

It's important to give them the chance to verbalize and express their concerns. Have them nod in agreement and say "Yes". Just by letting them express this fear, you're defusing the emotional impact it has on them. You're getting this psychological roadblock out of the way.

3) Make Them Recall Positive Reference Experiences

Have them remember a time when they were in a similar situation - where they bought something and then later were glad they did. Ideally something that five or ten years ago everyone in the industry purchased and that has now become an industry standard.

If you have an example like that, it'll also help to resolve the emotional stress of a buying decision.

Bridge the gap between doubt and trust

Sometimes the thing that prevents you from closing a deal is **lack of trust.** If they don't have the confidence that your product is the right choice for them, they won't feel comfortable to commit. Instead, they'll try to find a way out; they'll try to avoid making a decision. They'll try to avoid taking the risk.

Oftentimes it's not much that's missing.

If you sense a lack of confidence, make sure to sell on all three levels, address the elephant in the room and make them recall positive reference experiences.

Trust Trumps Transactions

Trust trumps transactions. We really learned this lesson when we were trying to get our first customers for our outsourced sales service.

Nobody will ever buy your product if they don't trust you. Everybody gets that in theory - but few people know how to use that in the sales process to close more deals. When we launched our outsourced sales company we used fake names. We were in stealth mode and didn't want others to know about our new venture yet.

So we had zero credentials, zero credibility, zero references, nothing but hustle. And we wanted other startups to pay us for selling their product in their name. That requires a lot of trust. How did we do it?

How could we build trust?

How could we get a company's CEO to give us the authority to represent their brand to outsiders?

We thought long and hard about this issue, until we came up with a solution:

Technology can solve this problem! We would operate totally transparent. We would record all our communication with outsiders. We would record our calls and emails, so our future customers could listen in and make sure we'd represent them correctly.

(This is the reason why all Business & Enterprise customers of our sales software now have automatic call recording).

So whenever we tried to sell our sales service to a startup, trust was indeed an issue. And boy were we ready to tackle that objection. "That's a great point, Mr Prospect! We want to make sure to have your full trust, so we'll operate fully transparent. We'll record every single call, and you can listen to any call recording you want at any time to check that we're doing a good job. Isn't that amazing? Don't you feel a lot better, now that you've heard that all calls are going to be recorded? I'm sure now you can trust us, right?"

Wrong!

They all heard it. They all liked it. Transparency is good. Control is good.

But on an emotional level, it didn't solve the issue they had to begin with. It didn't make them feel any different about our proposal. They still felt apprehensive about it, they still felt like it was too risky to give away their name to an outsourced sales organization to talk to their prospective customers. Even though they knew they could always listen in to these conversations.

Thousand Questions, One Issue

We had one specific customer - who became our second paying customer, and stayed with us for the longest time, from day one for almost two years.

Our first sales guy pitched them the idea on the phone.

Prospect: *"If you could actually deliver on your promise, we'd love it, but... we can't believe that you're actually going to do a good job, and we're afraid of that."*

Our sales guy: *"We're going to have transparency, you can listen to all the calls, don't worry."*

Prospect: *"Well, that sounds awesome... but we'll still need time to think about it."*

4 calls later... they still couldn't pull the trigger. I was chatting with our sales guy, and he said: *"This is crazy! We went through 4000 questions, I answered all of them, they really, really, really want to do it... but they just can't get over it. I don't know what to do. Now they sent us another 30 questions."*

We looked at all their objections and questions... and it all boiled down to one thing: trust!

They didn't feel comfortable, they were afraid, they didn't trust us.

So we got them on the phone one more time and said: *"Hey, for a moment, let's put aside all these technical questions. If we are honest to each other, you guys are simply not trusting us, and you're afraid that it's going to take too much time to coach, train, check and manage us. You're just afraid of all these things. We can argue this back and forth forever. But words will never make you trust us. Let's do this: Give us one week! We'll study your solution, and in exactly one week, on Tuesday at 9am, we will call you, the CEO, and we will pitch you on your product. We will make a cold call. You'll play a potential customer, we will play your company, and we will pitch you. And your job will be to be the most difficult prospect you could ever think of, ask the most difficult questions ever, and then let our actions speak louder than words. See how we react, see how we respond. See if we can sell you and convince you on buying your product. Because if we can do that, we can do it with anyone else."*

There was a moment of silent thinking from the CEOs end of the line, and then he said: *"Ok, let's do it."*

A week later we cold called him, sold him their solution and asked him: *"How did you feel about this call?"*

CEO: *"Let's get started. Let's do this. I feel really good about you guys."*

That's the power of building personal trust. Use your action to create trust, don't just ask for trust with words.

Trust > Transparency

Want to know what's crazy?

These guys, who had such a hard time trusting us in the first place never listened to a single call recording! Not even one single time. We had the logs. We knew exactly what they were looking at. They looked at the dashboards and our performance, but not even one time did they listen to one of the call recordings we shared with them.

Because the moment we created trust... we had it. And we never lost it. They never felt the need to listen in to one of our conversations.

The product had transparency to build trust. But the personal trust we created totally trumped that. In fact, in all our history with Elastic Sales, we did not even have a single customer who ever listened in to a sales call.

They all liked the idea of transparency. They all liked to have the option to listen in to our calls. But no one ever did. Because they trusted us on a personal level.

The 3 Levels Of Trust

Whenever you are selling a product for a company, you need to build three levels of trust.

You need to make them trust in your product. You need to make them trust in you. And you need to make them trust in your company.

What do you think is the first level of trust you must build in the sales process?

The personal level! First, they must trust you as a person. That's where you start. With the human being they are interacting with.

Then you create some trust in the product/service/solution you are selling.

And create some trust in the company that is behind the product and the person.

Trust always trumps transactions.

Give References That Sell

When you're talking with prospective clients, they'll sometimes ask you for references. They want to talk with someone other than you to get a real customer perspective on your product and service.

References of happy customers are one of the most powerful sales tools you have. You're basically turning your customers into an extension of your sales team. Use them at the right time, in the right way, and they'll close your most important **deals for you**.

The key thing here is to make sure you don't waste their time and burn them out on too many reference calls.

What's the best time to give a customer reference?

Late. It should be the last step in your whole sales process.

Keep your references close to the chest until your prospects are ready to buy, the deal is just about to happen and everything else is checked off the list.

Think of it as the final move to make the close. The prospect should have a sincere and strong buying intent and all the necessary information to understand the deal before you ever consider giving out a reference.

By offering them to speak with someone who already bought from you, you help them overcome any remaining fears or hesitations of making a bad buying decision.

Why not use your customer references early?

Your references are too precious to parade around. If someone is a happy customer of yours, they'll be willing to help you out by sharing their experiences with your prospects.

But keep in mind they have other things to do. If they're flooded with inquiries from your prospects, they'll turn sour. Don't burn out your happy customers by having them constantly talk to window shoppers who are too early in the sales cycle and later won't end up buying.

You want to shield your references as much as possible from failure. You don't want them to hear things like: *"Thanks for taking the time to tell us about your experience with company XYZ, we decided to go with another company though."*

You want them to be on team **winning** and get the validation that every person they talk to on your behalf becomes a customer. Everyone loves to hear things like: *"Thanks for sharing your experience with company XYZ with us; we're a happy customer now too!"*

The quality of the conversations your references have with prospects will also be a lot higher if you only let highly qualified prospects with a sincere buying intent talk to them. So make sure to only connect prospects and customers when it has the highest chances of success.

How do you tell prospects that you aren't willing to give them a reference yet?

Won't it alienate prospects? Make them feel like you have something to hide?

That's what sales people often worry about, but it's never what happens. Prospects will understand and respect you more for it if you decline to give them references too early but offer to do it later in the sales process.

Here's what you say when a prospect asks for a reference early:

*I'm happy to put you in touch with successful customers and give you references **at the right time**.*

I want to make sure that we first get to an understanding that this deal makes sense and is a good fit for both parties.

Once we've answered all questions and taken all the steps for you to be ready to buy, I'm happy to put you in touch with as many customers as you want before you actually end up signing the deal.

Sounds fair enough?

Your happy customers are like family. You wouldn't hand out your cousin's phone number to anyone just because they ask, would you?

If someone has sincere interest, they'll be ok with evaluating whether it's a good match or not before talking to references. In fact they will respect you even more because you're treating your customer references with respect and don't give them out prematurely.

By only letting references talk with people who are pretty much willing to buy, you create a virtuous positive feedback loop: Your references experience talking about your company as something positive & successful, and become stronger advocates of your brand in the process.

B2B Referral Sales

Every week I talk to startups that want to get more leads and are considering starting or expanding existing outbound sales efforts.

"How can we get more leads? Are we ready for outbound sales yet? How can we improve our cold calls?"

Have you ever thought about your existing customers as a great source for new leads? Yes, I'm talking about referrals from happy customers :) It sounds so simple nobody cares to actually do it right.

Referral sales can be your #1 source of new hot leads and turn into a massive growth engine for your B2B startup if you do it right. The funny thing is most startups don't do referral sales. And those that try do a half-assed job at it.

What does referral sales really mean?

Referral sales means closing your new and current customers on the concept of introducing you to other companies that are likely to need the solution you've built.

Why are referral leads better?

No outbound lead you could ever generate in any other form will ever have the same quality as referral leads. There are two levels of quality:

1) Your best customers will most likely know others who run very similar businesses, which means they are highly qualified leads for your company. &

2) You are being introduced to them via a friend and have the benefit of trust right at the start of the relationship.

Are referral leads still considered outbound leads?

Yes, they are. They were introduced to you, which is the warmest form of outbound sales you could ever do. However, it's still reaching out to someone who didn't come to you in the first place. If you're thinking of doing outbound sales you might as well start at the warmest point possible.

Why are so many sales people doing referral sales wrong?

Because they're afraid. It's scary to ask for more once you close a deal. Sales people worry that they might jeopardize a deal, or that it'll turn a positive conversation awkward. Go where others are afraid to go and you'll find massive opportunity. Don't let fear get in the way of winning.

When is the best time to ask for a referral?

Right after somebody made a purchase. I know that people like to wait until customers have been around for months. That's fine, but it's also a waste of time. Once someone decides to buy they are likely to be convinced enough to tell others about it. You should take advantage of this moment to grow your business faster.

The way most sales people try referrals:

They ask for a referral, the client says: "Yeah, let me think about it and get back to you later" and the salesperson replies: "Okay, thanks!" rather than pushing a bit further.

The right way to do referral sales:

1. Ask for a referral.

2. Anticipate the no (or "I'll think about it."). Ask one more time right then and there.

3. Make sure to give them an email template and make it easy and frictionless to actually make the introduction.

4. After you closed a referral, make sure that your new customer thanks the person who introduced you, so you're closing the feedback loop in a positive way (inspiring more referrals from the original referrer).

Referral Sales Script

You: *"Are you happy that you chose our product?"*

Customer: *"Yes."*

You: *"Great. Who else do you know who could benefit from a solution like ours?"*

Customer: *"Hmm... I'm going to think about this later and get back to you."*

You: *"I appreciate that, and I'm sure that over the months and years as you benefit more and more, we're going to get lots of referrals from you, which is going to be awesome. Today, let's take a minute right now and think about just one friend who is in a similar position and would really benefit from this."*

Some will tell you "No" in a slightly more annoyed way. That's ok. Just tell them "Okay, I respect that, I will follow up in an email, I really appreciate that you are offering your help." And just leave it at that.

Some will give you one or more names just because you pushed one more time (my experience has been that 40% of people will give you referrals after the second ask).

Write those names down and tell them: *"Great, thank you. I want to make it as easy as possible for you to make that introduction. So you'll get an intro-email from me. Just copy paste it and send it to Bob and Steve. Feel free to make edits or write something yourself if you like. Let's make this happen today!"*

Referral Intro-Email Template

Hey {firstname},

I wanted to connect you with Steli, their company does XYZ. I think this can be really interesting for you, and a contact would be mutually beneficial.

I'll let you guys take it from here,

Ben

After you close a referral

When you sign somebody up who was referred to you, ask them: *"Who is actually responsible for you getting all these benefits from becoming a customer of our product?"*

Many times you will get a response like: *"Uhm... who? You mean... you?"* And then you say: *"No, the person who introduced us in the first place..."* - *"Oh, yeah, Bob!"* - *"Do you mind doing me a favor and sending Bob a quick thank you email that he made a connection to us, so he knows that you appreciate it?"*

The moment they sent Bob the thank you email, you're closing the feedback loop, which will likely inspire Bob to make more referrals. The first thing Bob thinks when he gets that email is: *"Hmm, who else do I know that I could introduce this to?"*

Everybody wants to make successful connections and help others discover something they are grateful for. If you treat referral sales as a separate product that gets the same if not more attention from your sales team you'll see an ever growing amount of new hot outbound leads.

Make referrals part of every deal

Once you've seen success with referral sales you should make it part of the experience of buying your product and service upfront.

After you had the initial meetings and everything looks like the prospect is going to buy try saying this:

You: *"It seems like we're a great fit. I'm excited. Before we go any further exploring a potential deal I want to bring up that we're fully focused on building world class technology and on servicing and supporting our customers to massive success. What that means is that we're not investing in marketing and sales as heavily because our happy customers are referring us to others who could benefit from our product. Does that sound like a fair arrangement to you?"*

Prospect: *"Yes, that sounds fair."*

(I've never seen someone say *"No, I want you to spend less time on product and service and do more marketing and sales so I don't have to refer you to anyone."*)

Referral sales - the warm outbound lead generation growth engine

I've taught this system to hundreds of startup founders and many have implemented it to great success. But I have to warn you - it takes conviction to keep asking for referrals even if people say no at first.

It takes patience to ask again after someone fully rejects it. Just like anything in sales it needs the emotional stability to go on as you face failure in the early days.

If you can do that, you'll start a growth engine for your company that's going to support scaling sales for many years to come!

What about referral incentives?

I've found that in B2B you don't want to "pay" for referrals and that people are more likely to make them when they feel like they are providing value to their network without any selfish incentives.

Once in a while someone will ask for it and it's up to you to decide if you want to give people a discount or something else for helping you close new business. I personally think that's reasonable when asked but wouldn't offer it upfront.

SALES HIRING

Sales Hiring For B2B Startup Founders

During my sales office hours I often talk with B2B startup founders who are beginning to see success. They developed their product to a point where the few customers they have keep using it regularly. Their retention rates are okay and they have early signs of revenue growth.

It's time to ask the question: Should I hire salespeople?

Here are the four stages of sales hiring for B2B startups:

Stage #1: Founder-driven Sales (Founders only)

The first person to sell your product should be you, the founder, and your co-founders. Even if you hate sales and suck at it. Even if you don't have any sales experience and know-how. Do customer development yourself, and be as close to your prospects as you can.

Begin with the low-hanging fruit and tap into your network of
- friends and acquaintances,
- co-workers,
- past employers,

- alumni,
- and always ask for introductions left and right.

At this point the objective is not closing deals. Instead, focus on early stage sales exploration:

- Gain insights into your market
- Understand and listen to your customers better
    - What objections do they have?
    - How do they describe their problems?
    - What are their pain points?
    - How do they respond to your solution?
- Figure out which metrics truly matter for your sales outreach and your business
- Test different strategies, methods and tactics to make sales and drive business
- Get started with cold emails
- Learn sales hacking 101
- Write a sales phone script

This phase is all about getting your hands dirty in the startup hustle and figuring out what works in the real world. You're all about lean sales and validating your idea with the power of the hustle. The experience you gain will help you later evaluate salespeople. Watch this video to learn the basics of founder-driven sales:

http://bit.ly/2013pioneers

Stage #2: Founder-led Sales Team (2-3 Sales Reps)

Once you have some success (made some sales, generated some revenue) the question you will ask yourself is: "How do I grow this? How can I take this to the next level?"

This is challenging, because you still need to focus on developing your product further as well. Balancing these two responsibilities isn't easy.

Now is the time to hire your first sales reps. Don't hire expensive sales veterans here. You want them young and hungry. And hire two or three salespeople at the same time. It's about adding firepower to your sales efforts.

Why hire two sales reps at a time? Four simple reasons:

1. Friendly competition
2. Less dependence on individual performance
3. More data for future sales recruiting
4. More firepower

With two or three sales reps, you will be able to do a lot more, try out more things. It will energize all your sales efforts and add friendly competition.

Now you have a sales team - you're responsible and accountable for them. Sales thrives in this kind of competitive environment and team spirit. And staying afloat in an ocean of rejection will be a lot easier with a supportive team too.

When you tell your sales reps to try a new sales approach, it might work for one but not for the other. In that case you know that the sales approach is working, and the problem is with someone's ability to execute.

If you have only one sales rep, you don't really have anything to measure against. Two or three sales reps are still far from perfect for validating data, but it is a lot better than just one.

At this stage you still need to be deeply involved. You're managing and leading this team. You're still pitching, doing outbound, inbound, working with your sales reps, listening to feedback.

You can't outsource this. There are still too many critical decisions to be made. You need all these one-on-one experiences with customers, different sales channels and lead generation methods. It's not enough to monitor numbers. You need to be living them.

Goals you should accomplish before transitioning into the next stage:

- Try and test cold-email templates

- Use an effective sales lead management system
- Be experienced at negotiating deals and know how to handle discount inquiries
- Use drip marketing emails to convert leads better
- Have the ability to see early levels of predictability in your sales funnel

What about commissions/compensation?

Don't worry about setting up commission structures yet. It's too early. Hire these first 2-3 salespeople on a base level and work with them to get the sales process to predictability. Once you're there you can develop a commission structure with your sales team.

Read Aaron Ross's excellent book Predictable Revenue for some examples of how to develop your compensation structure with your sales team.

Stage #3: Junior Sales Leader (3-15 Sales Reps)

At this point your sales exploration has matured: results are a lot more predictable. You've established an effective sales funnel. You're generating consistent growth. It's not about exploration anymore – it's about time you start focusing on sales execution.

Let's bring in some experienced sales leadership: a sales manager or sales director.

What should this sales manager accomplish for your company?

- Fine-tune the rough sales approaches you've developed
- Expand on the things you've learned
- Grow and manage your sales team
- Set up quotas, train and coach your reps

You want to look for someone who has experience overseeing the growth of a tiny sales team of 3 people to 10, 20 or 30 people - because that's the next transition you're going to make. And it's one you don't want to be in charge of as a founder yourself.

Good sales managers will improve existing structures and optimize processes. They usually do not excel at building something from scratch and figuring things out. But they will propel your business forward if they can build on something that's already there.

Stage #4: Senior Sales Leader (25+ Sales Reps)

Once you're beyond that barrier of around 15 salespeople and you want to go really big, the next breakthrough will happen at 25+ sales reps.

You'll need a senior sales leader, a VP of Sales who could manage a few sales managers/directors. Someone with a proven track-record of scaling things big. Jason Lemkin shared some great advice on how to hire a VP Sales.[8]

A VP of Sales will work on sales strategy, scaling & expanding your sales channels & partnerships and move your customer base upstream as well as improving your unit economics. The VP will:

- build an org structure for the sales team
- develop hiring and training plans
- reorganize your commission structure
- groom sales talent to sales management positions
- open new offices
- add new channels like field sales to your inside sales team
- close larger deals.

It's hard – but it's worth it

Startup sales is tough. Nothing about it is easy. If you focus on the right things and hire the right people at the right time you're going to be able to see your startup go from sales exploration to sales execution and ultimately sales scale.

---

[8] http://blog.close.io/how-to-hire-your-first-vp-sales-and-not-screw-it-up

Final Word on Outbound Hustle

What you just learned in this book is practical sales advice from the trenches.

You learned how to get started selling your idea and sell products that aren't even built yet (and charge for it). You've learned how to make a cold call, how to send effective cold emails and what results to expect from these outbound sales efforts.

You've learned how to create a minimal viable pitch, how to manage any sales objection successfully and how to create a B2B sales referral engine for your company.

Everything you learned is highly practical and can be translated into your specific sales process within hours (not days, weeks or months)!

Now it's time to go out there and put these tactics to use. Leave your comfort zone and go create a successful outbound sales model that will empower your company to crush it.

Try our awesome sales software!

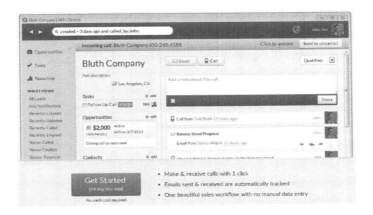

Over 2 years ago we started a "Sales As A Service" business called ElasticSales. The vision for Elastic was to build a massive sales infrastructure and empower startups and companies around the world to tap into that infrastructure in order to scale their sales efforts.

Think Amazon AWS for Sales.

Our mission was simple:

Never again should a great company fail because of a lack of sales.

We started hiring top sales talent, opening offices and signing up clients within the first few weeks. It was clear that there was massive demand for this service out there. What wasn't clear was what kind of software we would have to use to make this whole sales operation work smoothly.

We went out in the market to research the best technologies available and came back incredibly disappointed. Nothing out there was designed to actually help you sell more successfully.

All existing solutions seemed to be focused on the premise of turning sales professionals into manual *data-entry-monkeys*. None of them showed any understanding whatsoever of what a sales person's needs are when it comes to their job and daily workflow.

So after a lot of frustration we decided to fix the problem instead of complaining about it and we started developing our own internal sales application.

We lovingly called it **our secret sales sauce :)**

We knew nobody had ever been in a better position to develop next generation sales software since we had a few unfair competitive advantages:

- We had both salespeople and engineers

in the founding team

- We ran a sales outsourcing and consultancy firm for startups empowering us to test the software in all kinds of different use cases
- We had a clear and distinct philosophy and vision for the product

All that translated in a few simple principles when we started developing our software:

1. It had to be simple to use
2. It had to minimize manual data entry as much as possible
3. It had to be focused on the #1 priority in sales: good communication

We wanted to build software that sales people would actually love. We wanted to build something WE WOULD LOVE.

It took about 1.5 years of constant development and iteration with our internal development and sales team to realize that early vision and create something truly special.

During that time our sales people generated millions and millions of dollars in sales for hundreds of venture backed Silicon Valley startups using our secret sales sauce: Close.io

We knew we had a huge winner when we suddenly started to get more and more demand from other people who wanted to use our internal "secret-sauce-sales-software". At first we resisted (there is a reason you call it your secret sauce after all) but eventually we realized that it was the right thing to do to be true to our core mission:

>> Never again should a great company fail because of a lack of sales.<<

So we did it. In January 2013 we finally released Close.io to the world. And the response from the market has been incredible:

"Close.io is awesome! Moving over from Salesforce is mindblowing. I just wanted to see something and found it immediately. Funny how that's an advantage. Keep it up!" Joseph Walla, Founder & CEO, HelloFax

"The straightforward email and calling integration in Close.io helped us solve many of our workflow issues and increased our outreach by over 30%. This has caused us to achieve huge growth in revenues while doing less work!" Nick Persico, Director of Sales Operations, Krossover

"Close.io radically increased the number of calls

and emails to our leads by logging everything automatically so the reps can focus on talking not logging." Jeff Zwelling Co-Founder, Convertro & Co-Founder, EchoSign

Not too shabby right? :) Yes! Well... But how exactly does that affect you?

Let me tell you...

There are 4 reasons why Close.io will help you Close More Deals & Make More Sales:

1) You will make more & better calls

Make and receive calls with just 1-click. All calls are logged automatically. Lead activity information pops up as soon as the phone rings so the data you need is always at your fingertips!

2) You will send more & better emails

All your sales related emails are automatically tracked within the app no matter where you write the emails. You can see who opens your emails, save templates to improve your email workflow and keep all digital sales communication in one place without any manual work.

3) You can finally say NO to data entry

We hate data entry as much as you do, so we tried our hardest to help you avoid it. With auto-logging of calls, emails, and activity you can spend more time closing deals instead of entering data.

4) You can get answers to all your questions

The app collects most data based on your actual behavior and thus has not only more data but also more accurate sales data. We've built a powerful search platform that allows you to answer any question within seconds. Example? "Show me all leads in California with a 70 percent or greater chance of closing, whom I haven't called or emailed in the last week." Boom!

BUT IT'S NOT FOR EVERYONE!

Close.io is not for you if:

1. You are managing a pipeline of less than 100 leads per year
2. You are not using a phone or email to do sales
3. You work for a Fortune 500 Company

If you fall in one of these 3 categories you

SHOULDN'T BUY Close.io since it's not a good fit for you. Don't worry, if you email me and tell me this is not for you, I will personally send you recommendations for other sales software that will help you be more successful. I know them all. No problem.

In all other cases you seriously need to become a Close.io customer and see the immediate boost in sales success it will give to your startup.

Try Close.io now!

Want more startup sales advice?

http://close.io/free-sales-course

Questions, comments? Just contact me at steli@close.io I love to hear from you.

18088696R00096

MadeMade in the USA
San Bernardino, CA
28 December 2014